VANGUARD SERIES

EDITOR: MARTIN WINDROW

THE M47 & M48 PATTON TANKS

Text and colour plates by

STEVEN J. ZALOGA

OSPREY PUBLISHING LONDON

Published in 1982 by
Osprey Publishing Ltd
Member company of the George Philip Group
12–14 Long Acre, London WC2E 9LP

ISBN 0 85045 466 2

Filmset in Great Britain
Printed in Hong Kong

The M46 Patton saw its operational début during the Korean War. It was essentially similar to the M26 Pershing except for the engine and other improvements, and can be distinguished by the presence of large mufflers on the rear fenders. Here, a colourfully marked M46 of the 6th Tk. Bn. helps drag another Patton out of an irrigation channel near Chongpyong, Korea, 2 April 1951. (US Army)

Production

During the fighting in Germany in the last months of the Second World War, the US Army began receiving its first M26 Pershing tanks. Although referred to as 'heavy' tanks, the Pershings were in fact in the same class as the German Panther medium tank in terms of weight, armour and firepower. Following the war, the Army acknowledged that the Sherman was no longer viable as the standard medium tank when compared to more modern designs like the Panther, and the M26 Pershing was reclassified as a medium tank. With the intensification of the Cold War in the late 1940s the Army began a general modernisation of the armoured force. A rebuilt derivative of the M26 was accepted for Army service in 1948 as the M46 Patton tank. The essential element of the M46 programme was automotive modernisation consisting of a new CD-850 cross-drive transmission and AV-1790-5A engine. Although not realised at the time, this engine and transmission package would form the heart of American tank designs for nearly 35 years until the advent of the M1 Abrams in 1981. About 2,400 Pershings were eventually rebuilt to M46 Patton standards by 1951.

In 1948 the US Army authorised the initiation of a design programme for a family of three new inter-related tanks in the light, medium and heavy categories. The light and medium designs, T41 and T42, shared a very similar chassis, but the T42 mounted a heavier turret with a 90mm gun. Before the T42 pilot model was ready for testing, the Korean War broke out. The initial setbacks were a terrible shock to the US Army. North Korean T-34/85 tanks dominated the battlefield until adequate numbers of M4A3E8 Shermans and M26 Pershings could be scraped together and rushed to Korea. Although the M26 and M46 tanks proved easily capable of dealing with the T-34/85, the early North Korean successes and difficulties encountered by the US Army in

An M47 Patton of the 12th Regimental Combat Team advances through Dinkelsbuhl, Germany on 13 October 1955 during Exercise 'Cordon Bleu'. This is an early production vehicle with the initial turret grab-irons. The green-triangle-on-white-circle insignia is the traditional manoeuvre marking for 'aggressor' forces. (US Army)

mobilising enough tanks to send to Korea highlighted the decrepit state of the US tank inventory and the need for re-activation of medium tank production. Accentuating these concerns was the fear that another global conflict was imminent, leading to a frantic scramble to build tanks.

The T42 tank did not live up to expectations, being underpowered. However, the turret was better laid out than that of the M46, and it incorporated a sophisticated optical rangefinder. In September 1950, acting under extreme Congressional pressure, the Army decided to mount the T42 turret on a modified M46 hull and begin production of the new tank as the M47 Patton. While the American Locomotive Company and Detroit Tank Plant began to tool up for the M47, it was decided to modify the last batch of M26/M46 rebuilds with the same automotive improvements scheduled for the M47: the AV-1790-5B engine, CD-850-4 transmission, a new oil cooling system, simplified electrical harness and new brake controls. A total of 360 of these M46A1 Pattons were completed before M47 production began in April 1951.

The Army rashly assumed that the M47 Patton merely consisted of mating a proven new tank turret with a well-tested chassis. Inadequate testing resulted in a tank plagued by technical problems, which were exacerbated by the frenetic production schedule. Inadequate supplies of the M12 optical rangefinder delayed issue of M47s, and the 1st and 2nd Armored Divisions did not begin to receive them until 1952. No M47 Pattons served during the Korean War, but the M46 Patton was employed with distinction by the 6th and 64th Tank Battalions. Production of the M47 continued through 1953, by which time 8,676 had been built. The M47 was clearly a stop-gap vehicle. It was the last major medium tank design to retain the anachronistic fifth crewman (assistant driver). Its only major improvement over the M46 was its more sophisticated fire controls, and the better ballistic shape of the turret and glacis plate. Even before it entered production the US Army contracted Chrysler Corporation in Decem-

An M48 of the 66th Armor crosses a pontoon bridge over the Cumberland near Ft. Campbell during Exercise 'Quick Strike' on 13 April 1960. The M48 is easily distinguished from later vehicles of the series by the external .50cal. machine guns on the commander's cupola. (US Army)

ber 1950 to develop its replacement, the M48 Patton.

The new M48 was to retain the same engine and transmission as the M47, and the suspension was very similar, although a wider track was developed. The major aim of the design team was to develop a better armour layout and to incorporate a larger diameter turret ring. The assistant driver was omitted and the armour layout was derived from work on the M103 heavy tank. As in the case of the M47, the apocalyptic fears of the Cold War led to over-hasty production schedules without adequate testing. The first M48 pilot model was designed and built in only one year, and the first production vehicle which rolled off the assembly lines in April 1952 came from the brand new plant at Newark, Delaware, where ground had first been broken only 14 months before. Production was supposed to amount to 9,000 M48s by July 1954, but serious technical problems in the original production batches—as well as the arrival in 1953 of the Eisenhower administration, with its less frenzied view of the world situation—led to this plan being considerably scaled down. The GAO later reported that 'Initial production vehicles were defective to such an extent that they were not even acceptable as training vehicles'. The Army claimed that many of the problems that persisted with the M48 were due not to any inherent technical defects but to poor maintenance and crew inattention.

The M48 was introduced into service with the 2nd Armored Division in 1953, and in 1955 the M47 was declared 'limited standard'. Its service career was thereby rendered rather shortlived, and of the 8,676 manufactured, all but a few hundred were exported under the Military Assistance Program (MAP). The M47 formed the backbone of the NATO tank force for nearly 15 years.

The M48 was followed by the M48A1 after about 3,200 had been built. Nearly identical to the M48, it had in place of the exposed, remote-control .50cal. machine gun mount a completely enclosed .50cal. gun in an M1 cupola.

The M48 and M48A1 Patton's greatest tactical deficiency was its short range of only 112km. While

An M48A1 of 37th Armor, 4th Armd. Div. takes part in Exercise 'Wintershield II' near Allersberg, Germany on 3 February 1961. The M48A1 was the first tank of the series to be fitted with the distinctive M1 commander's cupola. This particular tank is fitted with the Universal Jettison Fuel Tank Kit on the rear to extend its effective range. (US Army)

actually a bit better than its contemporaries, such as the Centurion, it made necessary the use of a jettisonable rack on the hull rear which could carry four 55-gallon fuel drums to extend the range outside the combat area. This shortcoming was eliminated with the introduction of the M48A2 in 1955. The M48A2 incoporated a new version of the engine, the AVL-1790-8, which offered better fuel economy through the use of fuel injection. The M48A2 also had a new rear engine deck which cut down on its infra-red 'signature' and permitted the use of larger fuel tanks, which combined with the engine improvements doubled its range over the M48A1. Many of the M48 and M48A1 tanks were exported through MAP, and the M48A2 became the standard US Army and US Marine tank of the late 1950s and 1960s. It was the most widely manufactured version among the total of 11,703 M48 Pattons of all models which were built by the time production ceased in 1959. During the production run of the M48A2, it was decided to replace the troublesome M13A1 stereoscopic rangefinder with a more easily operated M17C coincidence rangefinder. This feature, along with other fire control improvements, was adopted on the M48A2C. The only external difference between this variant and the earlier M48A2 was the absence of a small return roller between the last roadwheel and the drive sprocket.

Operation of the M47 & M48

Driver's Controls

The adoption of a cross-drive transmission on the M47 permitted the use of very simple driver's controls. A manual control lever was located to the driver's right, and by moving it forward or back the tank could be shifted from neutral to low, high or reverse gear. By moving it to either side in any of the four gears, it could be steered. Acceleration and braking was accomplished by conventional foot pedals. The advent of the M48 brought with it completely redesigned controls like those of an automobile: steering was by means of a steering wheel and gear changing was done with a gear lever attached to the steering column on the right side. Although these controls necessitated a sophisticated transmission, they permitted an ease of driving unmatched in any tank of the period, and training was greatly simplified. The steering system also proved a great deal more reliable than earlier hand-levered brake steering, even though the system was more complicated.

Fire Controls and Armament

While there was some variation in fire control details through the M47-M48A2 series, the basic elements were similar. The only major difference was that in the M47, the gunner controlled the rangefinder, while in the M48 series, it was controlled by the commander. The gunner sat in the right forward half of the tank turret with the TC (tank commander) immediately behind him and the loader on the other side of the gun in the left half of the turret. The gunner's controls were located on a fire control assembly with a right handed pistol grip. The operation of the hydraulic turret traverse was accomplished by turning the pistol grip clockwise for a right traverse, and anti-clockwise for left traverse. Moving it down or up elevated and depressed the gun. The use of hydraulic traverse in the M47 and M48 in place of earlier mechanical or electrical drives gave it the fastest turret traverse of its day, though the system required more maintenance. There were manual controls at the left of assembly in case the hydraulic system failed. To the right of the fire control assembly was an azimuth indicator to show the gunner the direction in which the turret was pointed relative to the rest of the tank, and behind this was the ballistic computer. The gunner's main sight was a 6 × periscope with illuminated

Tankers of 1st Platoon, Co.'D', 3rd Medium Tk. Bn., 35th Armd. Regt. are briefed near their M48A1 tanks outside Beirut airport on 14 August 1958. These Pattons, along with Marine M48s, were used during peacekeeping operations in Lebanon in the summer of 1958. The jettisonable fuel drums are evident on the rear of tank '13'.

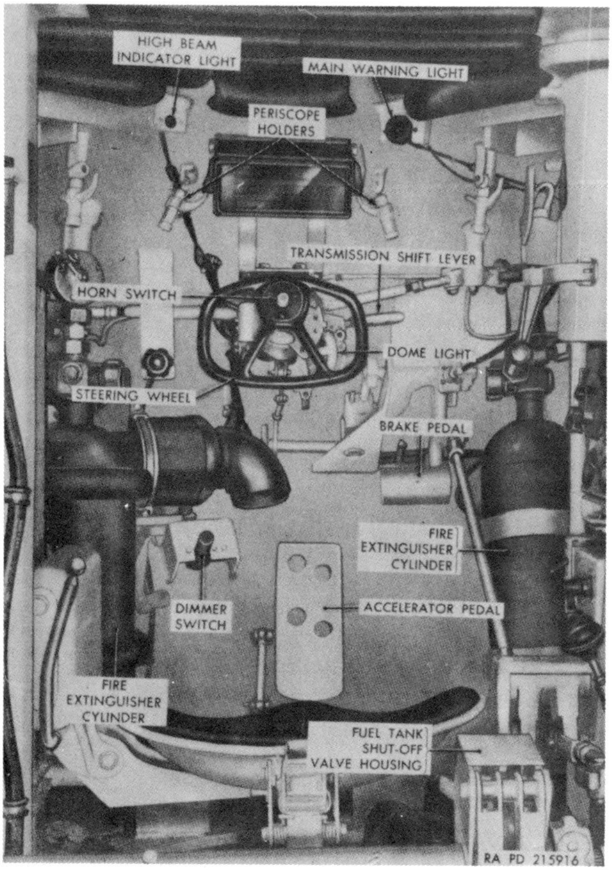

Driver's compartment of the M48.

reticles, but a secondary telescopic sight, not linked to the computer or rangefinder, was also provided.

The TC had a control handle very similar to that of the gunner, and he could override the gunner's control to traverse the turret and elevate the gun. On the M48 series, he was responsible for operating the optical rangefinder and was provided with a separate periscopic sight for surveillance.

The loader stood or sat on the other side of the breech, and in front of him was the co-axial machine gun and its ammunition stowage and feed system. The M47 carried 71 rounds of 90mm ammunition of which 11 rounds were carried vertically around the left wall of the turret basket in ready racks, and the remainder in racks under the basket floor. The M48 series carried slightly fewer rounds (M48:60, M48A2:64, M48A3:62), but they were more conveniently located. To the left of the driver were 19 rounds in tubular racks, and to his right a further 11 rounds. There were 16 rounds stowed vertically in front of the loader on the basket side, eight rounds in a bin on the floor and eight more behind the loader in the rear turret bustle.

The M36 90mm gun in the M47 and the M41 90mm gun in the M48 series could fire a wide range of ammunition types, and ammunition stowage was dependent on the type of mission to which the tank was assigned. In the 1950s and 1960s the US Army put a great deal of reliance on HEAT shaped-charge rounds, since they could penetrate any armour then in use. Such rounds are relatively slow and have a pronounced ballistic arc in flight as compared to the flatter trajectory of kinetic energy rounds, and this was a major factor in adopting a complicated rangefinder which permits more accurate use of HEAT rounds. A typical firing sequence against an enemy tank would take place as follows:

The TC would spot an enemy tank through his 6 × periscope, and, using his control grip, swing the turret to engage the target. Instructing the driver to stop, through the earphones and intercom, he would turn over the turret controls to the gunner and instruct the loader what type of ammunition to chamber. On hearing these instructions, the gunner would actuate the ballistic computer

Using the rangefinder on the M47 and early M48s was called 'flying the geese', as a pair of 'V'-shaped illuminated reticles had to be stereoscopically aligned. This simulated view shows the appearance of the reticle, the range read-out and the ammunition read-out (HVAP-T) at the bottom of the image.

An M48A1 of Co. 'F', 40th Armor (Berlin Brigade) stands watch on Friedrichstrasse (Checkpoint Charlie) in Berlin during the October 1961 crisis. This particular vehicle carries a bulldozer kit and a VSS-1 searchlight. This overhead shot clearly shows the prominent engine deck grill-work of the early M48 series. (US Army)

handle to select the correct type of ammunition, and would disengage the super-elevation crank until the TC had made the ranging adjustments. The TC would switch to the 10 × optical rangefinder, make the ranging measurements with the proper controls, and inform the gunner that he was finished. The gunner would re-activate the super-elevation crank, which would automatically result in the range information being transmitted by mechanical linkage to the ballistic computer. The computer in turn would depress the gun line of sight in the gunner's periscope, necessitating the gunner to elevate the gun barrel to put the target back into the crosshairs. This procedure put the proper amount of super-elevation into the gun, and the gunner would fire. The whole operation took about 15 seconds and gave about a 50 per cent probability of a first round hit at 1,500 metres, which was truly remarkable for its day. During close-range engagements the system was not used, with the crew either substituting manual input of an estimated range, or simply using the co-axial machine gun for ranging and targeting for a faster response.

The main drawback of the stereoscopic rangefinder was the skill required to operate it. Each commander had to set the diopter and inter-pupillary scales to match his own eyesight, and over 20 per cent of crews did not have adequate vision to use the rangefinder properly. To speed the operation the TC could set the range knob for the estimated range. When first looking into the sight the TC would see two illuminated reticle patterns in a V-shape. Using his controls, the two V-shapes had to be superimposed—a procedure known as 'flying the geese'. In spite of training programmes, and the great potential of the system, results of the fire controls in actual use were often disappointing; and in the mid-1950s the US Army decided to adopt coincidence optical rangefinders instead. First used on the M48A2C, these required more light to operate properly and were marginally less accurate, but they were a great deal easier to use. With a coincidence rangefinder the target appears as a ghost image to the left and a true image to the right. When both images are superimposed the proper range has been found, in much the same fashion as cameras are focused.

An M48A5 of the 50th Armd. Div. (National Guard) during summer manoeuvres at Camp Drum, NY in 1980. This vehicle is an M48A5 (Low Profile) with the Urdan commander's cupola and twin M60 pintle-mounted machine guns on the roof. (Midic Castelletti)

Cupolas

A peculiar feature of the M48A1 and later models of the Patton was the use of the M1 commander's cupola. It was not popular, as the machine gun was very difficult to reload and the firing solenoid was frequently broken while entering or leaving the turret. During the Vietnam War many Patton crews removed the cupola machine gun and mounted an M2 .50cal. externally on the cupola roof. The Israelis thought even less of the system, attributing their high commander casualties in part to the need for the TC to expose himself to see properly, thus placing him in a very high and vulnerable position. By 1973 most M48s in Israeli service had the M1 cupola removed and replaced with an Urdan cupola similar to that on the early M48, but with provisions to hinge the hatch so that the commander could swing it partly open, leaving the hatch over his head for partial protection from airbursts.

Replacement and Retrofit

The US Army was fairly content with the M48A2, but the arrival of the T-54 series in the Soviet Army prompted the US Army Tank and Automotive Command to initiate design studies of a tank with a heavier main gun. This was the T95 programme beginning in 1954. The T95 incorporated many technical novelties, but proved too complex and expensive to produce and was terminated under Congressional pressure. In its place the Army decided to up-gun the M48 with the new British L7 105mm, fit a diesel version of the existing engine, and make other hull improvements. In 1959 this resulted in the M60 tank. The decision to switch to diesel fuel was part of an overall Army programme which included dieselisation of the M113 APC and the M109 and M110 self-propelled howitzers. Diesels offer better fuel economy and a reduced fire hazard in combat. Although the M60 closely resembled the M48A2, there were extensive detail changes ranging from new roadwheel designs through to new fenders, simpler armour layout on the hull front, and many internal improvements.

Initiation of M60 production in 1959 signalled the end of M48 production, but not further development of the family. In 1959 it was decided to modernise the old and troublesome M48A1s by rebuilding them with M60 components like the AVDS-1790 engine, new engine decks, and the improved fire controls of the M48A2C. These vehicles were designated M48A3. They closely resembled the M48A2, but had top-loading aircleaners on the rear fender and a slightly different grill pattern. Towards the end of the modification programme the last batch of vehicles had additional improvements carried out including hydraulic brakes, improved steering, a new inflatable turret seal, metal screening on the rear turret stowage basket, and a G305 turret cupola vision riser offering the TC better 360° vision. These vehicles, serial numbers 601W to 726 W, were called M48A3 (Late Model).

In the mid-1960s, there was a plan to retrofit older M60s with M60A2 guided missile gun launcher turrets, releasing a number of 105mm gun turrets. Prototypes were built mounting these turrets on M48A3 hulls, and these vehicles were to be designated M48A4. Delays in the M60A2 programme resulted in the project being cancelled, however. Although no M48A4 tanks were actually produced, the US Army occasionally uses the M48A4 designation for administrative purposes in referring to Israeli-modernised M48A2s which have AVDS-1790 diesel engines and M68 105mm guns provided by the US.

By the early 1970s the Army had replaced its M48 tanks with M60s and M60A1s, retiring most M48A3s to the National Guard or the Marines. Serious production delays in the M60A2 programme, and inventory depletion due to large shipments of M60A1s to Israel in the wake of heavy tank losses in the 1973 war, left the US Army short of battle tanks at a time when the Soviet Union was greatly increasing its own tank force with T-62s. As an inexpensive expedient until M60A1 production proved sufficient, it was decided to modernise mothballed M48s, M48A1s, M48A2s and most M48A3s to bring them up to M60 standards. These new vehicles were called M48A5. The extent of the rebuild varied enormously, with the early M48s requiring a whole new engine and major fire control reworking as well as the new 105mm gun and associated features. The conversion on the M48A3 was less extensive, requiring the new M68 gun, new ammunition racks, a new turret basket, T142 track and other improvements. The initial vehicles (serial numbers A3001 to A3999) used the M1 cupola with G305

Key, M48A5 gunner's controls:
(1) Gunner's traversing handle. (2)/(3) Inset: Gunner's traversing handle showing firing control (2) and magnetic brake switch to allow control to function (3). (4) Manual elevation control. (5) Manual firing release. (6) Manual firing control. (7) Turret power pressure gauge. (8) Telescope reticle illumination switch. (9) Telescope controls. (10) Gunner's elevating handle.

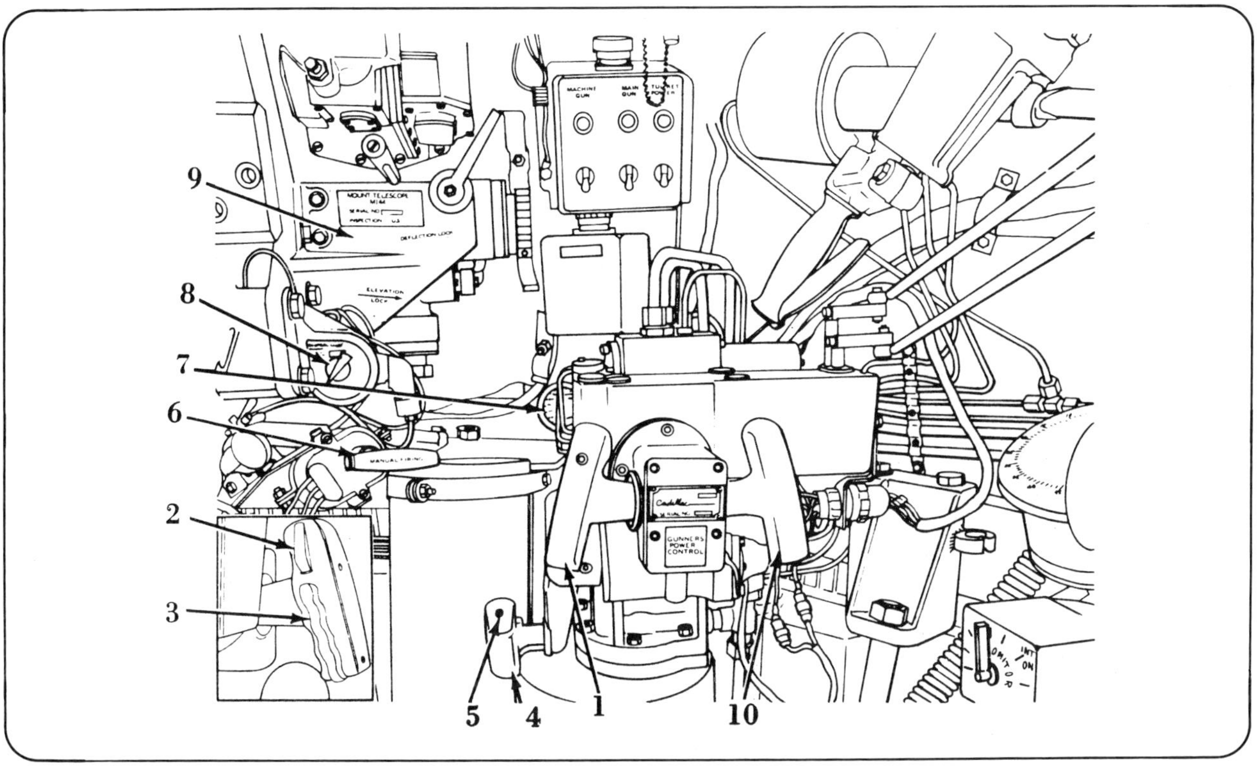

Israeli dissatisfaction with the M1 commander's cupola led to the development of a low-profile cupola similar to that first employed on the M48, but without the external machine gun cradle assemnly. This has been manufactured by Urdan and is used on Israeli, American and some exported Pattons. (George Balin)

turret riser, but the later vehicles, called M48A5 (Low Profile), used an Israeli-manufactured Urdan TC cupola reminiscent of the old M48 type, two M60D 7.62mm pintle-mounted external machine guns and the later 2D engine. There were 2,050 of these conversions carried out by the Anniston Depot, of which about 1,600 were intended for the Army National Guard and for tank battalions in Korea. American rebuilt M48A5s have also been exported, and conversion packages have been sold to a number of allied countries for their own modification programmes.

The most recent derivative of the Patton family is the XM246 DIVAD, which consists of a new turret mounted on an M48A5 hull fitted with twin L70 Bofors 40mm cannon and a fire-control radar system. The US Army plans to add over 600 of these to its inventory by the mid-1980s. (Ford Aerospace)

Besides the tank version of the Patton series, there are three major derivatives. The AVLB (Armored Vehicle Launched Bridge) is a turretless Patton with a hydraulically operated bridge implacement system used for gapping small ditches or streams. The M88 is the armoured recovery vehicle version of the Patton, and is fitted with a fixed superstructure, an A-boom and related winch equipment. The XM246 DIVAD (Divisional Air Defence) is an M48A5 with a new turret designed by Ford Aerospace mounting twin 40mm Bofors guns and a fire control radar. The US Army plans on acquiring 618 DIVADs to replace the aged M163 Vulcan, and it is expected to enter service in the mid-1980s.

Operational Employment

Austria

The Austrian Army received 152 M47s which were used to form the 4, 7 and 14 Panzer Bataillon in the late 1950s. The 4 and 7 Pz. Bn. were re-equipped with M60A1s in the 1960s, and the last battalion will be converted over to M60A3s. The Austrian Army has been scrapping the hulls but emplacing the turrets on concrete pedestals along the border to form pillboxes.

Belgium

The Belgian Army received 784 M47s in the 1950s, which were used to equip its cavalry regiments until the Leopard I became available in the 1970s. Small numbers are still in service.

Ethiopia

The Ethiopian Army deployed two companies, amounting to 30 M47s, during the 1977 war with the Eritrean guerillas in the Ogaden desert war. About 24 were destroyed in the fighting.

Federal Republic of Germany (FRG)

The Bundeswehr was the first and largest recipient of M47 and M48 tanks. In the early 1950s it received 1,120 M47s, and later received 203 M48A1s, 1,001 M48A2s and 462 M48A2Cs. These tanks were used to form 16 tank brigades. As the

newer-model Pattons were received the older tanks were passed on to other NATO countries such as Turkey. The Bundeswehr currently has about 1,064 M48s, these being mainly M48A2s and M48A2GA2s. (The latter is a modernised M48A2 with 105mm gun and other improvements carried out by Wegmann & Co.; about 650 have been so modified.) The M48s serve mainly in the territorial units and will gradually be sold off or provided as foreign aid to other NATO countries as the Leopard II becomes available. The M48 has proved very influential in German tank design, and the Leopard I shows obvious signs of this.

France

Along with the Bundeswehr, France was among the first recipients of M47s, receiving 856 in the 1954–56 period. These formed the basis of French armoured divisions until the AMX-30 became available in the 1960s. The French were the first to use the M47 in combat, when the 8e Regiment de Dragons was landed in Egypt during the Suez crisis of 1956. They saw little fighting. The French M47s were gradually withdrawn from service, and many ended up as range targets.

The USA supplied Austria with M47s to equip three battalions in the 1950s. Most of these were retired from service with the advent of the M60A1, but their turrets were dug-in along the Austrian frontier as pillboxes. (Austrian Army)

Greece

The Greek armoured force is made up primarily of M47s and M48s. In the 1950s 300 M47s were delivered through MAP, and in subsequent years Germany provided at least 30 more. The US provided 673 M48 and 102 M48A1; and of these about 170 are currently being modernised to M48A5 standards and 600 to M48A3 standards, using American parts.

Iran

Iran received about 400 M47s in the late 1950s from the US. In 1970–72 a tank modernisation facility was set up at Masjed-Soleiman to modify Pattons for Iran, Pakistan and Jordan. The modified M47s are called M47M and the pro-

The M47 formed the heart of the new *divisions blindées* of the French Army in the 1950s until the arrival of the AMX-30. In keeping with a long-standing tradition dating back to the Char B battalions of the 1930s, some French tank regiments named their vehicles after towns, in this case 'Notre Dame de Lorette' of the 501e RCC. (Pierre Touzin)

gramme includes substitution of an AVDS-1790-2A diesel engine, CD850-6A transmission, replacement of the bow gunner's position with additional ammunition stowage, and many other small detail improvements. All of the Iranian vehicles were so modified as well as about 147 Pakistani M47s. Plans for further work on Jordanian M47s did not come to pass owing to the overthrow of the Shah and Jordan's backing of Iraq. During the 1980 Iran-Iraq war, M47Ms took part in the fighting, and it is believed that any such vehicles captured by Iraqi forces will eventually be turned over to Jordan.

Israel

In 1960 the Israeli government attempted without success to obtain M48 tanks from the United States to balance the arrival of large numbers of T-54 tanks in the Egyptian and Syrian arsenals. The US government was unwilling to supply these, but agreed to a secret transfer of about 200 M48A2 and M48A2Cs from the Bundeswehr to Zahal as part of Germany's reparations programme. These arrived until 1964, when press leaks forced the German government to halt the transfers. However, the US government relented and began modest shipments of its own. The Israelis decided to re-arm the M48 with 105mm guns, but by the outbreak of the 1967 war only about one company of tanks (15–20 vehicles) were so equipped. During the war two Patton battalions were attached to Ugda Tal in the Sinai campaign: the 79th Tank Battalion commanded by Maj. Ehud Elad, and serving in the 7th Armoured Brigade, and another battalion attached to Col. Uri Barom's special Task Force. Zahal intentionally refrained from using Pattons on the Jordanian front due to the fact that the Royal Jordanian Army was equipped with the same type of vehicles.

The M48 was a popular tank in Zahal, being more reliable and faster than the Centurion and being easier to maintain. It had better hull armour than early models of the Centurion (120mm -vs- 76mm), but thinner frontal turret armour (110mm -vs- 152mm). The Centurion was generally felt to be better armoured as a larger percentage of hits are registered on the turret during tank-vs-tank fighting, and the turret stowage bins on the Centurion offered a certain measure of stand-off protection against infantry anti-tank rocket launchers. The least popular feature of the Patton was the M1 cupola, as mentioned earlier. The M48 was successfully employed in the 1967 fighting, with the Patton battalions spearheading the attack of Ugda Tal through the Gaza Strip. During the fighting around the Rafah junction Barom's battalion smashed over a dozen T-34/85s and 15 IS-3M heavy tanks. One of the most bitter fights in which the M48 was involved took place at Jiradi, where the Israelis lost several tanks to mines and anti-tank guns but managed to overwhelm a well entrenched defensive position. The commander of the 79th Tank Battalion and several of his officers were killed in this battle.

Many of the M48s and M48A1s supplied to Greece in the 1950s are now being modernised to M48A3 and M48A5 standards. (Pierre Touzin)

An M47 of 11.Panzer-Division crosses a Class 60 pontoon bridge near Regensburg, Germany on 2 February 1961 during Exercise 'Wintershield II'. (US Army)

By the time of the 1973 war American arms policy had changed, and Israel was supplied with about 900 M48s and several hundred M60A1s. Many of the M48s were re-equipped with AVDS-1790 diesel engines and M68 105mm guns. A programme was also started to replace the M1 cupola with the low-profile Urdan cupola. The M48 battalions formed the backbone of Israeli armoured formations in the Sinai theatre, while the Centurion battalions were committed to the Golan fighting. The M48s were able to deal with Egyptian T-55 and T-62s on even terms due to the modernisation programme and in the hands of the well trained and highly determined Israeli crews the tanks of Zahal enjoyed a very decided edge. Tank losses in this sector were very heavy, however, due in part to the early successes of Egyptian infantry using 9M14M Malyutka anti-tank missiles and RPG-7 grenade launchers. After the heavy tank commander losses on M48s in 1967, Israeli Patton commanders had been taught to fight 'buttoned up'. However, this made them very vulnerable to infantry anti-tank teams, and the tactics were soon changed. Increased emphasis was placed on the turret crew using roof-mounted .30cal. machine guns to spray likely missile team hiding places, and in the last days of the war tank losses to missiles dropped dramatically.

Italy

Italy received 2,480 M47s in the 1950s; these formed the basis of two armoured divisions and a number of armoured cavalry regiments. The M47 was the major battle tank of the Italian Army until the 1960s when the M60 and Leopard I gradually began to replace it. There are still several hundred M47s in Italian service, though they are being phased out in favour of newer types.

Japan

Japan received a single M47 for evaluation purposes. The Japanese Self Defence Force found it to be unsuited to the smaller stature of Japanese crews, and began development of the Type 61 tank, which bears more than a passing resemblance to the M47.

Jordan

By the time of the 1967 war Jordan had been supplied with 396 Patton tanks, consisting of 49 M47s equipping the 12th Independent Armoured

▲The Bundeswehr was supplied with both M48A2s and M48A2Cs, and this side view of an M48A2C shows the slight difference between these models—the absence of a trailing idler wheel between the last roadwheel and the drive sprocket. This Patton has the features added by the Bundeswehr, including the large rear turret stowage box, an AEG Telefunken searchlight and smoke mortars. (Pierre Touzin)

Many of the Bundeswehr Pattons have been converted to the M48A2GA2 version by Wegmann; the most obvious external signs of the modifications are the 105mm gun and the new commander's cupola. The rear engine deck of the M48A2 closely resembles that of the later M48A3 and M60, but lacks the large air filters on the fender and has more extensive grill-work on the hull roof. (Pierre Touzin) ▼

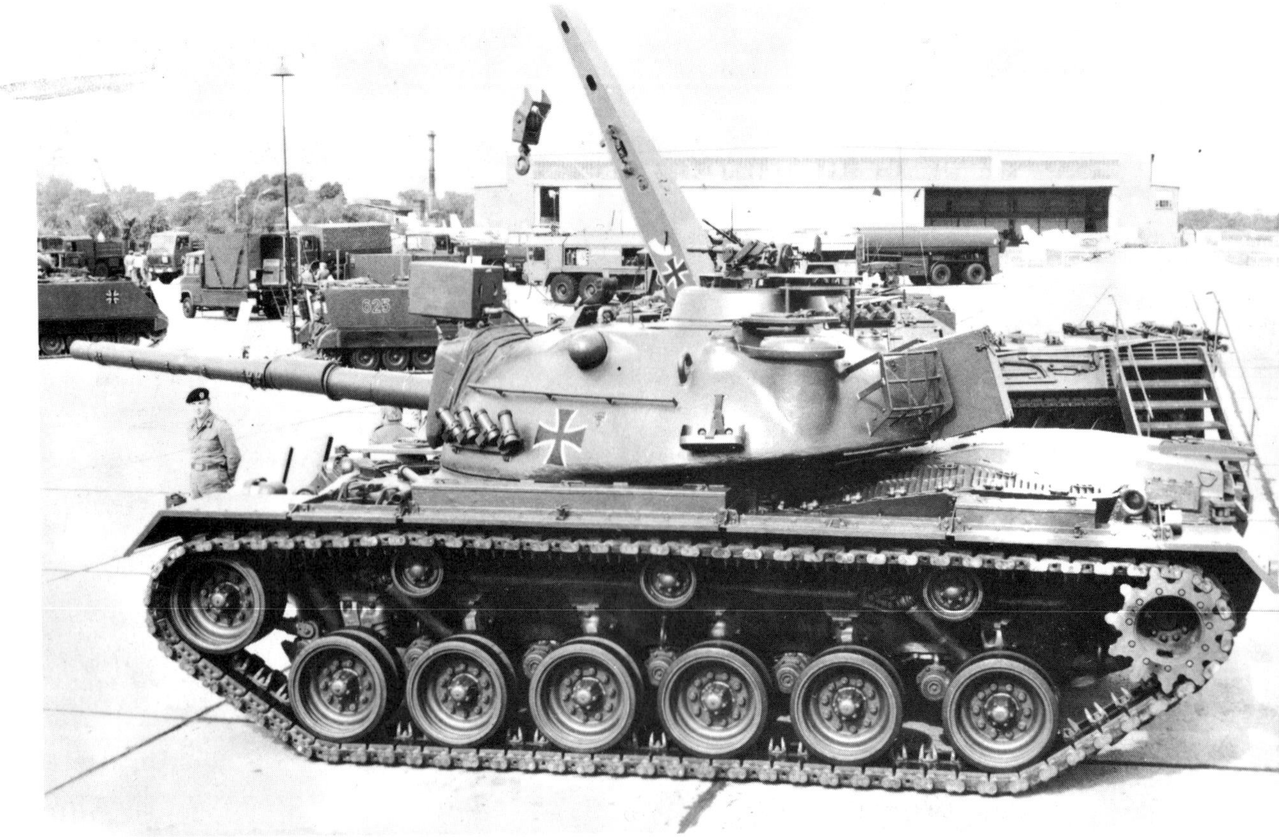

Regiment, and 197 M48s and 100 M48A1s equipping the four regiments of the 40th and 60th Armoured Brigades. The composition and commanders of these units in the 1967 fighting were:

12th Ind. Armd. Regt. (Lt. Col. Saleh Aliyaan)

40th Armd. Bde. (Col. Rakan Anad Jazy):

- 2nd Armd. Regt. (Lt. Col. Saleh Abdullah Suhair)
- 4th Armd. Regt. (Maj. Merzouk Aashwi)

60th Armd. Bde. (Col. Sherif Zeid bin Shakir):

- 3rd Armd. Regt. (Lt. Col. Alawi Jarrad)
- 5th Armd. Regt. (Maj. Kalef Awwad)

When the fighting broke out between Israel and Jordan on 5 June 1967 the 40th Armd. Bde. was in its staging area near the Damiya bridge, and the 60th Armd. Bde. was near Jericho. Initial Israeli attacks against Hebron in the south prompted the Jordanians to begin moving the 60th Armd. Bde. towards Hebron and the 40th Armd. Bde. to Jericho, but heavy attacks on Jenin in the north led to this order being rescinded at the end of the day. The result of this fruitless movement was that the two brigades spent most of the day in transit along narrow mountain roads subjected to repeated Israeli air-strikes which knocked out many tanks. Without respite, the 40th Armd. Bde. was sent on a 100-mile trek back towards Jenin and the 60th made a forced night march to Jerusalem. By the early morning of 6 June the 60th Armd. Bde. was reduced to less than half strength, but on reaching Elzariya it launched a counter-attack against the Israeli 10th Mechanised Brigade. The fighting cost the Jordanians about a dozen tanks, and by afternoon further air attacks had claimed more casualties and the 60th Armd. Bde. was ordered to withdraw over the Jordan River, bringing with it only six M48 tanks.

In the northern sector the town of Jenin was covered by the 12th Armd. Regt., which positioned 'B' Sqn. south of Birkin, 'A' Sqn. near Ya' Abad and 'C' Sqn. in reserve, each squadron having about 15 M47s. An attack near Birkin on the afternoon of 5 June by the Israeli armoured

The Israeli Zahal began receiving M48A2C Pattons from Germany and the USA before the outbreak of the 1967 war. This vehicle is evidently from a Bundeswehr shipment, judging from the headlights. The Pattons served in two battalions of Ugda Tal during the 1967 Sinai fighting. (Israeli Army)

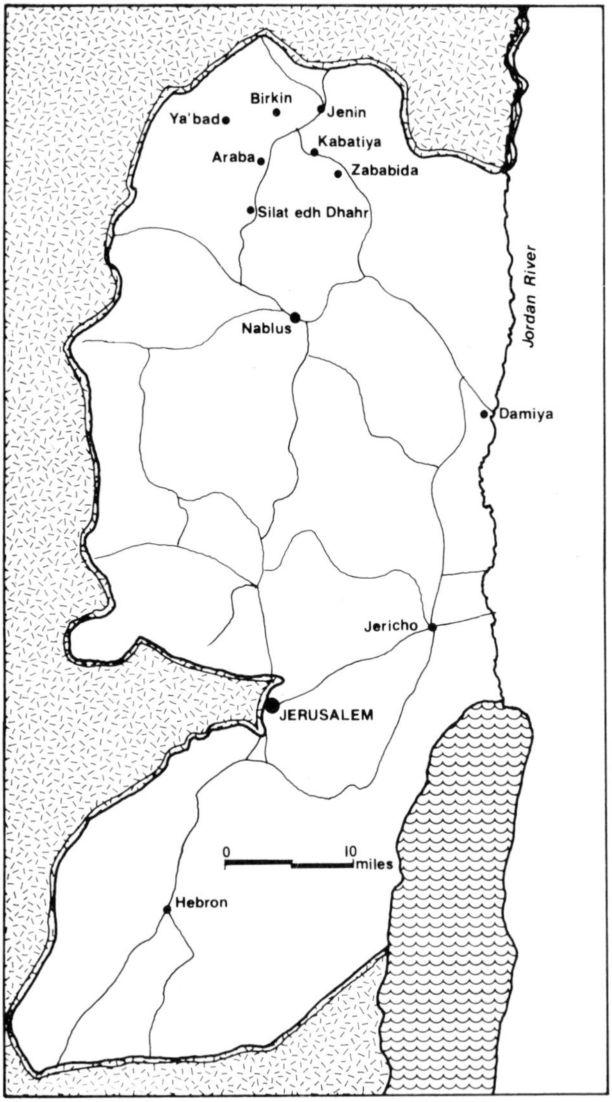

West Bank of Jordan, 1967

brigade commanded by Bar Kochva was hit by 'B' Sqn., which claimed several Shermans before an air strike knocked out three M47s. Continued Israeli pressure led to 'C' Sqn. being committed to the fighting around Birkin, and the Jordanians claim to have knocked out 18 Israeli tanks in the fighting that ensued. The 12th Armd. Regt. was pounded for the rest of the day by Israeli air-strikes, and again engaged Israeli tanks in the early morning hours of 6 June. The remnants of the unit withdrew to Kabatiya around dawn with only eight M47s remaining. By this time, elements of the 40th Armd. Bde. were arriving to reinforce this sector. The 4th Armd. Regt. moved on Jenin, while the 2nd Armd. Regt. moved on Araba. About two companies of M48s of the 4th Armd. Regt. attacked Jenin, hitting a half-track engineer unit and rear service elements and causing severe casualties. By nightfall air-strikes and battles with Israeli Shermans had worn the force down to seven M48s, which then withdrew to Zabadia, and were overwhelmed by an Israeli armoured attack on 7 June. The left flank of the Jordanian positions at Araba held by the 2nd Armd. Regt. were pushed back to Silat Edh Dhahr and Nablus. The positions at Nablus were eventually crushed by an enveloping attack by a battalion of AMX-13s and a battalion of Centurions, and only eight M48s escaped over the Jordan River.

Total Jordanian tank losses in 1967 were 171 tanks, of which about 40 were Centurions of the 10th Ind. Armd. Regt. which was wiped out by air strikes near Hebron. The remainder were the M47s of the 12th Armd. Regt., which was nearly totally wiped out around Jenin, and the M48s of the 40th and 60th Armd. Bdes. Many M48s knocked out by air strikes on 5 June were recovered and are not included in these totals. The Israelis considered the Jordanians to be the best tankers of any Arab army they faced in 1967, and on more than one occasion Israeli tanks units were only saved by the air force. Indeed, Jordanian tankers consider their main foe to have been the Israeli air force, and attributed most of their losses to this cause. The Israelis acknowledged losing 112 tanks in Jordan, mostly to the Pattons, and an equal or larger number of half-tracks. Following the war, Jordan was partly resupplied with Pattons, bringing its strength back to 283 M48s. There were plans to rebuild these at facilities in Iran in 1979, but the fall of the Shah put an end to this scheme. The Jordanians will probably dispose of their M48s in the 1980s as part of an agreement with the US by which they will receive M60A1s and M60A3s in return.

Korea

The Republic of Korea has two armoured brigades and seven independent battalions made up mainly of Pattons. They originally received 531 M47s, of which about 250 are still in service. In addition they received 140 M48A1s, 280 M48A2Cs and 50 M48A3s. Most of the M48s are now being brought up to M48A3 standards, and some to M48A5 standards. The latter are interesting in that they

are being fitted with side skirts and have had a unique Jonell fire control/night vision system added.

Morocco

Morocco has three Patton battalions, and has received 114 90mm M48s and 65 M48A5s. These tanks do not seem to have taken a large part in the fighting against the Polisario Front in the contested former Spanish Morocco area.

Norway

The Norwegian Army received 38 M48 tanks in the 1950s, which no longer play an important rôle in the Norwegian force structure.

Pakistan

The first real combat test of the Patton tank came in 1965 during the short Indo-Pakistani War. In the mid-1950s, Pakistan's cavalry regiments began receiving some 230 M47s and 202 M48s, and many tank officers were sent to the US Army Training Center at Ft. Knox. At the outbreak of war in 1965 Pakistan had about 15 armoured cavalry regiments, each with about 45 tanks in three squadrons. Besides the Pattons, there were about 200 M4 Shermans re-armed with 76mm guns, 150 M24 Chaffee light tanks and a few

M48A2C Pattons of 1st Co., 79th Tk. Bn., 7th Armd. Bde. probe their way through Rafah Junction in 1967. The success of the 79th Tk. Bn. at Rafah was a key ingredient in the rapid drive through Sinai in 1967. (Israeli Army)

independent squadrons of M36B1 tank destroyers. Most of these regiments served in Pakistan's two armoured divisions, the 1st and 6th Armd. Divs.—the latter being in the process of formation in 1965.

The Indian Army of the time possessed 17 cavalry regiments, and in the 1950s had begun modernising them by the acquisition of 164 AMX-13 light tanks and 188 Centurions. The remainder of the cavalry units were equipped with M4 Shermans and a small number of M3A3 Stuart light tanks. India had only a single armoured division, the 1st 'Black Elephant' Armd. Div., also called 'Fakhr i Hind' ('Pride of India'), which consisted of the 17th Poona Horse, the 4th Hodson's Horse, the 16th 'Black Elephant' Cavalry, the 7th Light Cavalry, the 2nd Royal Lancers, the 18th Cavalry and the 62nd Cavalry, the two first-named being equipped with Centurions. There was also the 2nd Ind. Armd. Bde., one of whose three regiments, the 3rd Cavalry, was also equipped with Centurions.

During the 1967 war only one company of Pattons had been re-armed with 105mm guns; by the 1973 war most had been so modernised. This Patton has the new gun, the reduced commander's cupola, and an AVDS-1790 diesel engine, as is evident from the presence of the large air filter box over the fourth and fifth return rollers. The .50cal. machine gun mounted on the gun mantlet is used for training. (Israeli Army)

Objective assessments of the 1965 war are as yet largely unavailable, and what Indian and Pakistani accounts do exist are as often as not poisoned by propaganda and highly suspect. Particularly contentious are the various claims for enemy tanks destroyed and so forth. The ostensible cause of the war was continuing friction over the Jammu and Kashmir section of north-east India. The Pakistani Army had been training and equipping Muslim guerillas in the area, leading India to respond by probing attacks along the border. In late August 1965 India seized the strategic Haji Pir Pass, and the escalating border incidents reached a crescendo on 1 September when the Pakistani Army, including elements of the 6th Armd. Div. advanced into the Chhamb—Akhnur area. The Pakistanis hoped to lure the nearby Indian 1st Armd. Div. into the region between the border and the Chenab River so that the Indians would have to fight with the mile-wide river to their back. The Indians had no intention of accepting this fool's errand, and decided instead to launch a series of blows against Pakistan, the main attacks being in the Lahore and Sialkot sectors.

The thrust against Lahore consisted of the Indian 4th Inf. Div. supported by the three tank regiments of the 2nd Ind. Armd. Bde.; they quickly advanced across the border, reaching the Ichhogil (BRB) Canal by 6 September. The Pakistani Army held the bridges over the canal or blew up those it could not hold, effectively stalling any further advance by the Indians on Lahore. Sensing an opportunity to envelop and destroy the Indian formations, the Pakistani 1st Armd. Div. was sent to the area south of the main Indian incursion around Kasur with the aim of advancing along the rear of the Indians' left flank, trapping them against the BRB Canal. The Pakistani advance was hampered by the necessity for elaborate bridging operations over the canal and the Rohi Nala River, with the lead elements of the division arriving at Khem Karan on 7 September. The Pakistanis immediately began probing attacks against the Indian positions, which were not executed with any particular vigour and were brushed back. A reconnaissance in force by Pattons and Chaffees towards Mahmudpura on 8 September was ambushed, and several tanks were lost in a flooded plain. The scope of the probes made it clear to the Indians that a major attack was forthcoming, but realising that the terrain favoured the defender, they withdrew under light pressure to prepare a trap.

The area north of Khem Karan consists of well-irrigated plains crossed by many waterways, dykes and other channels. The fields were high in sugar cane and other crops, and the plains could easily be flooded by breaching irrigation canals to render the terrain unsuitable for mechanised advance. Four Centurion and Sherman squadrons were positioned to cover key roadways and approaches, forming a horseshoe into which the Indians expected the Pakistanis to march. The other squadrons were broken up into troops, with two troops assigned to the bridges over the Rohi Nala in the north in case the probes by the Pakistani 12th Cavalry should prove to be more than feints, and another troop allotted to the 4th Inf. Div., which formed the first line of defence in the village of Asal Uttar. The 4th Inf. Div. was well equipped with jeep-mounted 106mm recoilless rifles, bazookas and other close-range anti-tank weapons, and the area to the division's rear was well covered by both artillery and the tank squadrons. The commander of the 2nd Ind. Armd. Bde., Brig. Thang Raj, issued strict instructions to his tank crews to wait until the Pakistani tanks had approached quite close to their hull-down positions before opening fire so as to take best advantage of the concealment offered by the thick sugar cane crop.

Pakistani efforts until 9 September had been desultory and ineffective as the division awaited the arrival of the last of its troops. Indian air attacks failed to destroy many tanks, but succeeded in destroying a supply train which left most of the Pattons with only 30 rounds of ammunition and limited fuel for the forthcoming offensive. On Friday 10 September 1965, Maj. Gen. Nasir Ahmad Khan ordered his 5th Armd. Bde. forward. Indian artillery and small arms fire clipped away what little infantry support the Pakistani Pattons had, leaving the tanks exposed to Indian anti-tank teams. The Pattons charged ahead, in spite of the poor visibility due to the cane. The Pattons were visible to Indian recoilless rifle and tank crews who could see the swaying of the cane as the enemy approached and the upperworks of the Pattons' turrets. The Indians soon began to exact a heavy toll from the Pakistani tanks, striking them from the front and side. As casualties mounted, one Pakistani regiment tried to skirt the defences by attacking the town from the east, but soon found itself bogged down in a plain flooded

The AVLB is a scissors bridge mounted on an M48A2 hull for use in crossing anti-tank ditches and other obstructions. This particular Israeli AVLB was photographed while on manoeuvres in the Sinai in 1971. (Israeli Army)

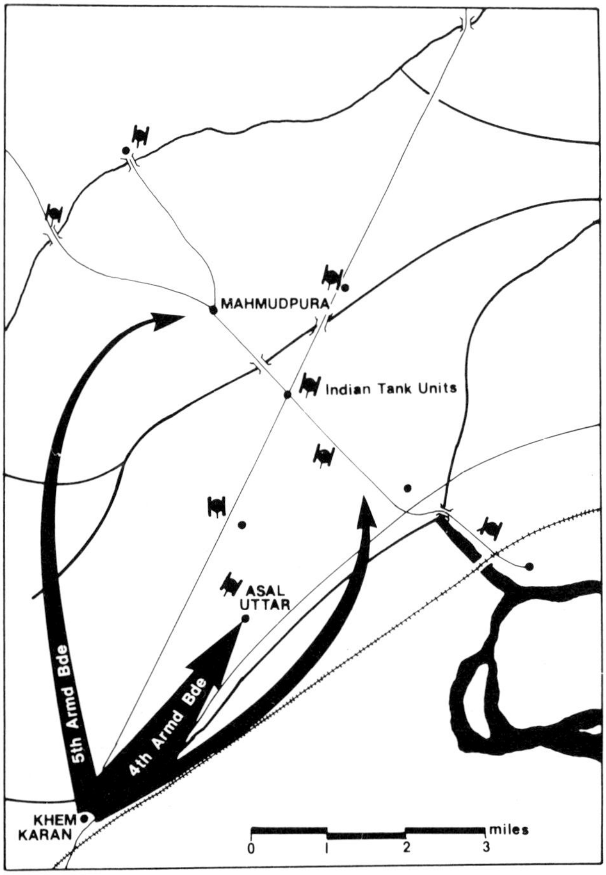

Battle of Asal Uttar, 10 September 1965

by a breached nullah. What Pattons did fight their way through the village found themselves faced by a cordon of stationary, concealed tanks and artillery and were quickly decimated. By 1330hrs the 5th Armd. Bde. attack had petered out with terrible losses. The 4th Armd. Bde. was ordered to attack the Indian right flank by a drive on Mahmudpura, but the Indians had foreseen this move and had flooded the area. The Pakistani attack became bogged down and came under intense artillery and tank fire. The Indians intercepted the following communication between the brigade's commander and the divisional commander (GOC):

BC—It's not possible for us to advance any further due to stiff resistance. Heavy enemy shelling has completely pinned us down.

GOC—It is most important that the advance is continued. Therefore, in the name of Islam, Pakistan and Hillale Jurat, I command you get up and go forward.

BC—I will do my best but as things are I do not know how the hell I am going to do that. This bloody enemy artillery is knocking the hell out of us and I am afraid at the moment that I can't do any better than this.

GOC—Move forward to your objectives forthwith.

BC—I cannot move; Indians are ahead of me.

GOC—Come and see me immediately.

BC—Where do I come? I don't know.

GOC—Move straight on and turn right.

BC—Do you know where I am? If I turn left the Indians get me, if I turn right the artillery gets me. Where do I come and how?

GOC—Turn right till you hit the road, follow it and you will find me at milepost 36.

The brigadier never found him, but a pair of jeep-mounted recoilless rifles, of the Indian Army did, destroying the tank of Maj. Gen. N. A. Khan and killing all its crew. By nightfall the ten square miles around the Khem Karan—Asal Uttar battlefield were littered with 97 Pakistani tanks, more than 65 of which were M47 and M48 Pattons. The area became known as the 'Patton Nagar'—'Patton Graveyard'. Besides the heavy losses in equipment, the Pakistani 1st Armd. Div. lost its commanding general, one brigadier and six regimental commanders either dead or captured. The Indians claim to have lost only 12 tanks during the fighting on 10 September 1965.

The crushing defeat of the Pakistani 1st Armd. Div. and the inability of the Indian Army to vault the BRB Canal stalemated the Lahore front. The Indians turned their attention to the main thrust,

The Israelis singled out the Jordanians as being the toughest tankers they faced in the 1967 war, particularly during the engagements around Jenin. This M48A1 served with the 40th Armd. Bde., as is evident by the square red/yellow insignia on the right fender. (Jordanian Army)

This Korean M47 is from the later production batches fitted with a T-shaped muzzle brake. (George Balin)

called Operation 'Nepal', in the Sialkot sector. The aim of the attack was to seize the key Grand Trunk Road around Wazirabad. The striking force of the Indian 1st Corps was the 1st Armd. Div. supported by the 14th Inf. and 6th Mountain Divisions. The infantry seized the border area on 7 September; realising the threat, the Pakistanis rushed two regiments of their 6th Armd. Div. from Chhamb to the Sialkot sector to support the Pakistani 7th Inf. Div. there. These units, plus an independent tank destroyer squadron, amounted to 135 tanks: 24 M47 and M48 Pattons, about 15 M36B1s and the remainder Shermans. The majority of the Pattons belonged to the new 25th Cavalry commanded by Lt. Col. Nisar, which was sent to the Chawinda area.

The Indian plan was to drive a wedge between Sailkot and the 6th Armd. Div., which it believed was stationed around Chawinda. In fact there was only a single regiment there at the time. The Indian 1st Armd. Div.'s drive quickly divided, with the 43rd Lorried Inf. Bde. supported by a tank regiment attacking Gat, while the main blow of the 1st Armd. Bde. was hurled against Phillaura. Pakistani air attacks caused moderate damage to the tank columns, but exacted a heavier toll on the lorry columns and infantry. The terrain features of the area were very different from those around Lahore, being quite dusty, and the approach of the Indian attack was evident to the 25th Cavalry by the rising dust columns on the Charwah-Phillaura road.

The lead elements of the Indian drive fought their way into Phillaura, but were pushed back out towards Gadgor for a loss of 15 tanks. Both sides licked their wounds for two days, engaging in

Many of the Korean M48s and M48A1s are currently being modernised to M48A3 and M48A5 standards. This battalion is colourfully marked with yellow lightning bolts and pennants, white numbering and a sand/olive drab camouflage scheme. (Aris Pappas)

Although not successful on the Lahore front, M47s of the Pakistani 6th Armd. Div. proved very effective in the fighting in Chhamb and in the Sialkot sector during the 1965 war. (Col. M. A. Durrani)

sporadic infantry forays and artillery duels. The next attack on 11 September was spearheaded by the 17th Poona Horse commanded by Lt. Col. Tarapore. The Centurions were brought under fire by recoilless rifles and tanks, and the command tank was knocked out. The skirmishes between the 25th Cavalry and the Poona Horse lasted 12 hours, and in the dust and chaos it became difficult to distinguish one side from the other. The Indians made the ludicrous claim of 67 Pakistani tanks destroyed, which was well in excess of the total number in the area at the time. The outnumbered Pakistani forces were obliged to withdraw to Chawinda, where they awaited the next attack. On 13 September, the Poona Horse and Hodson's Horse began combined infantry-tank attacks against Jassoran. The engagements lasted for two days, with the climactic battle being fought on 16 September, when the Poona Horse supported a Gharwal Inf. Bn. attacking the small village of Butur Dograndi. The Indian tank attack was broken up by Maj. Raza Khan's 'C' Sqn., 25th Cavalry supported by Pakistani anti-tank teams firing Cobra missiles. The commander of the 17th Poona Horse, Lt. Col. A. B. Tarapore, was killed when his second command tank was hit, and the attack faltered. Both sides had suffered heavy losses in the fighting, and confined their attacks to infantry and artillery barrages until the ceasefire on 23 September. Two British journalists who visited one of the Patton squadrons of the 25th Cavalry after the ceasefire counted 25 burned-out Centurions in a three-mile stretch near Chawinda even after the Indians had begun retrieving destroyed vehicles. Of these, 11 were in a field no more than 800 yards across—a grim testimony to the intensity of these encounters. The Pakistanis admitted losing 44 tanks in the Sialkot sector, but claimed 120 Indian tanks, and the British journalists saw no reason to doubt them.

Following the war India admitted losing 128 tanks, and this probably consisted of about a dozen in the Lahore sector, a similar number in the Chhamb area, and the remainder in the Sialkot sector. The Pakistanis admitted losing 165 tanks, more than half of which were knocked out in the débâcle at Asal Uttar. These losses are probably on the low side, but many tanks damaged in combat were later retrieved and put back into action. Both sides claimed in excess of 400 tank kills on the ground and about 100 from air attacks, which is clearly excessive.

1: French M47, 8e Régiment de Dragons; Suez, 1956

2: South Korean M47, DMZ, South Korea, 1974

A

1: Portuguese M47, Mecklenbourg Cav.Regt., 1st Ind.Mixed Bde., 1978

2: Italian M47, Divisioni Corazzate 'Ariete', 1972

B

1: Iranian M47M, Khuzestan front, 1980

2: Pakistani M47, 1st Armd.Div.; Asal Uttar, 1965

C

1: Jordanian M47, 'C'Sqn., 12th Tank Regt.; Jenin, 1967

2: Belgian M47, 6e Régiment de Lanciers, 1967

D

1: Pakistani M48, 6th Armd.Div.; Sialkot sector, 1965

2: Spanish M48A1, Regt.Alcazar de Toledo; Spanish Sahara, 1974

1: Israeli M48A2C, 7th Armd.Bde., Ugda Tal; Sinai, 1967

2: West German M48A2C, Pz.Btn.364, 12.Pz.Div., 1978

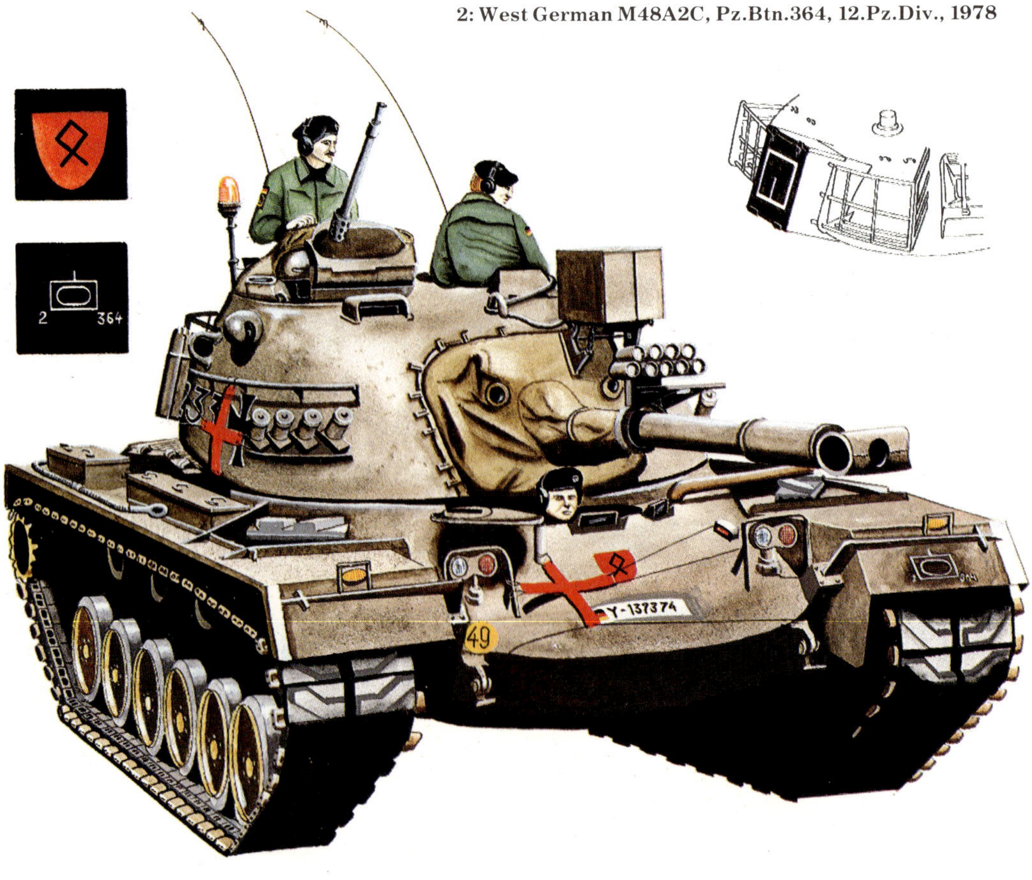

F

1: USMC M48A3, 1st Marine Tk.Bn.; Vietnam, 1968

2: US Army M48A3, 1st Bn., 69th Armor; Vietnam, 1969

G

1: USMC M48A3, 4th Marine Tk.Bn.; Fort Irwin,CA, 1980

2: South Korean M48A5 (Korean Pattern); Seoul, 1980

H

The Patton emerged from the Indo-Pakistan War of 1965 with a tarnished reputation. The fiasco at Asal Uttar was the obvious source of this disparagement, though a contributory factor was the exaggerated esteem in which the Patton had been held by both the Indian and Pakistani soldier before the war. Yet no vehicle, whatever its technical merits, can survive the kind of gross tactical bungling which characterised the Pakistani charge into the tank trap at Asal Uttar. Much attention has been paid to the supposed advantages of the Centurion over the Patton in these encounters, ignoring the fact that the majority of Patton casualties were caused by recoilless rifles, artillery and anti-tank guns, and that a third of the Pattons lost were simply abandoned due to lack of fuel and ammunition. In the Sialkot sector outnumbered Pattons performed exceedingly well in the hands of the 25th Cavalry and other regiments of the 6th Armd. Div., which exacted a disproportionately heavy toll of Centurions from the Poona Horse and Hodson's Horse. The Indian Army has made much of the fact that some of its Centurions survived repeated hits; yet have failed to point out that the majority of tanks in the Sialkot sector were Shermans whose guns were inadequate even in 1944. Neither the Indian nor Pakistani Army showed any great facility in the use of armoured formations in offensive operations, whether the Pakistani 1st Armd. Div. at Asal Uttar or the Indian 1st Armd. Div. at Chawinda. In contrast, both proved adept with smaller forces in a defensive rôle such as the 2nd Armd. Bde. at

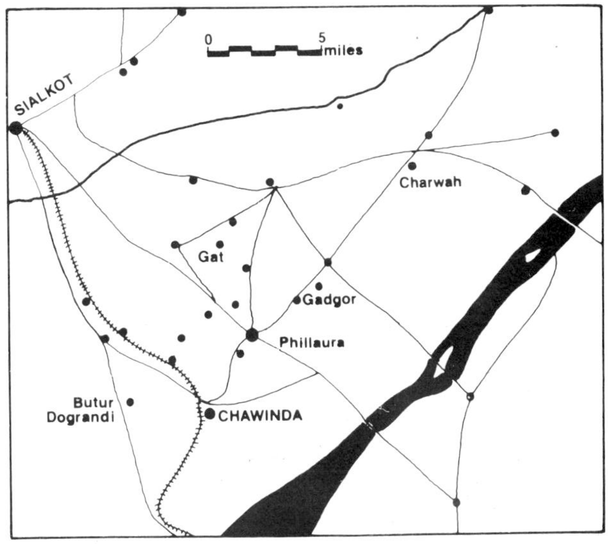

Battle of Chawinda, September 1965

An M48 of 25th Cavalry advances near Chawinda during the 1967 war. The 25th Cavalry had two squadrons of M47s, while 'C' Sqn. was equipped with M48s. (Col M. A. Durrani)

Spain's M47s were modernised by Chrysler España with a conversion package developed by the American firm of BMY, who originally developed it for Iran and Pakistan. The conversion replaces the bow gunner with additional ammunition stowage, improves the fire controls, and adds an AVDS-1790 diesel engine. These vehicles are called M47E or M47s ('España' or 'Spain'). (US Military Attaché—Spain)

Asal Uttar and the 25th Cavalry at Chawinda, where they defeated their better equipped but clumsier foes. The M47 and M48 did not play a major role in the 1971 war.

Portugal

Portugal was originally supplied with about 161 M47s, of which only about three companies (34 tanks) are still in service with the Mecklenbourg Cavalry Regiment. Recently, Portugal also received 30 M48A5s, mainly from the USA but from Germany as well. Portugal is a likely recipient of further M48s from Germany.

Saudi Arabia

Saudi Arabia originally received about 23 M47s from the USA and eventually acquired another 108, probably on the international market. While no longer in Saudi service, some of these tanks have been turned over to allied Muslim states such as Somalia (25) and Sudan (17).

Spain

The Spanish Army received 389 M47s in the 1950s as part of an American arms package tied to the lease of airbases in Spain. These replaced outdated PzKpfw IV tanks which had been supplied by Germany in 1943, and formed the basis of the Brunete Armoured Division. In the early 1960s these were joined by 65 M48s and 66 M48A1s, which were used by the Regimiento Alcazar de Toledo. One Battalion from this unit was sent to the Spanish Sahara in 1974, when there was a flare-up of troubles in the area. These tanks have been modified to M47E and M48E standards by the addition of AVDS-1790 diesel engines by Chrysler España, and other modifications similar to those carried out on the Iranian M47Ms.

Switzerland

Switzerland received two M47s in the 1950s for trials, but decided to produce a tank of its own—the Pz61—which was obviously influenced by the M47 and M48.

Taiwan

The Chinese Army has about 100 M47s and 175 M48s acquired partly from the USA and partly on the open international arms market.

Thailand

During the flare-ups in 1979 along the Thai-Kampuchean border, the USA rushed 50 M48A5s to the Thai Army to bolster it against border incursions by the North Vietnamese Army.

Tunisia

Tunisia received a single company of 14 M48A3

tanks and a few M88 recovery vehicles in the 1960s.

Turkey

Turkey was among the largest recipients of American MAP aid, receiving 1,347 M47s from the USA and from Germany, 1,849 M48s and 350 M48A1s. Some of the M47s saw combat action against T-34/85s and Marmon-Herrington armoured cars in the hands of Cypriot forces during Operation 'Attila', the invasion of Cyprus in August 1974. Turkish forces are currently in the process of being modernised with American and German help, with the Germans providing modification kits for about 200 M48s, and the USA recently selling 348 kits to bring M48A1s up to M48A5 standards.

Yugoslavia

The Yugoslav Army was supplied with 319 M47s in the 1950s in accordance with the US policy of balancing Soviet arms sales to Tito with American aid. This led to the peculiar situation of M47s and M48s serving alongside T-34/85s and T-54s!

United States

The first deployment of Patton tanks in combat by US forces came in July 1958 when M48s of the Marine 3rd Medium Tank Battalion were landed in Lebanon as part of the US peacekeeping effort. They saw no serious fighting, and later in the summer were joined by the Army's 3rd Tank Battalion, 35th Armor, which shared in the occupation duty. In May 1965 Marine Pattons were again landed as part of the US force during the Dominican Republic crisis.

On 9 March 1965 the first Marine M48A3 Pattons of the 3rd Tank Battalion landed at Danang, South Vietnam. This was the first US tank unit in Vietnam and would be joined by the

During the 1979–80 crisis along the Thai-Kampuchean border, the US rushed about 50 new M48A5 Pattons to Thailand; these were the first M48A5s exported. This particular vehicle is an M48A5 (Low Profile). (Thai Army)

Marine 1st Tk. B., a year later. The first Army tank unit to arrive in the war zone was the 1st Sqn., 4th Cavalry in 1965, serving with the 1st Division. Initially, the Army showed little enthusiasm for the deployment of tanks in Vietnam, feeling that they were unsuited to the terrain and the type of unconventional war being fought there. However, experiences with 1st Sqn., 4th Cavalry revealed that tanks were useful in supporting mechanised infantry operations and a host of other rôles. Eventually three Army tank battalions would serve in Vietnam: 2nd Bn., 34th Armor; 1st Bn., 69th Armor; and 1st Bn., 77th Armor, all with M48A3 Pattons. In addition there were numerous Pattons serving in the Armored Cavalry Squadrons. Initially, regimental armoured cavalry squadrons contained a tank company with three platoons of five tanks each and two command tanks, one with a dozer blade. These formations were later reorganised, and in 1969 the Pattons began to be replaced with M551 Sheridan light tanks. The tank battalions had 54 Pattons in three companies of 17 tanks (three platoons of five tanks and two tanks in the HQ section) and three tanks in the battalion HQ section. Frequently these battalions were committed piecemeal, with companies assigned to various infantry units or to security duties.

Tank tactics in Vietnam reflected the unconventional nature of the war. The Patton provided heavy firepower to bolster infantry actions, or could be used to repulse road ambushes on convoy duty. Tank companies would sometimes be assigned to aid in base defence, where their canister rounds could cause a Viet Cong assault to wither. The principal enemy of the tank in Vietnam was not other armour, but mines, which accounted for over 75 per cent of the tank casualties. The other main threat was from infantry anti-tank weapons like the RPG-7.

Although not designed for this style of warfare, the M48A3 proved as suitable as could be expected. It was a rugged and durable vehicle and could survive all but the largest mine blasts. The average mine would usually blow off one forward roadwheel and some track, and an especially large mine might knock off several wheels and damage the torsion bar housings. If parts were available the tank would often be running by the next day. The Viet Cong eventually began using aerial

Turkey has one of the largest remaining fleets of M47s in NATO, some of which saw service in Operation 'Attila'—the invasion of Cyprus—in 1974. (Pierre Touzin)

During the 1965 Dominican Republic crisis Marine tanks like this M48A3 were faced by rebels equipped with Swedish L60s and French AMX-13s, but little fighting ensued. (USAF)

bombs for mines; for example in 1966 near Cu Chi, an M48A3 of 1/69th Armor hit a 500lb mine that blew off the rear end and the entire engine, though the crew miraculously survived. The M48, like any tank, was vulnerable to RPG-7s. Some tanks absorbed multiple RPG-7 hits and kept fighting, but a single hit could sometimes ignite stores or ammunition, immediately disabling a tank and its crew.

The substitution of M551 Sheridans for Pattons in cavalry units in 1969 was not popular. The Sheridan was poorly protected against mines due to its thin armour and often suffered the death of the driver and serious internal fires. Nor did it have the weight or power needed to crush its way into dense foliage like the Patton. One variant of the Patton used by the Marines in Vietnam was the M67A2, which was an M48A3 mounting an M7-6 flamethrower and a 378-gallon fuel tank. The flamethrower fired through the false main gun barrel; it had a range of 180 to 200 metres and a duration of 60 seconds between refills. The Army preferred using M132 'Zippos', which were M113 APCs with the same flame equipment.

There was only a single instance of tank-vs-tank combat between US and NVA forces in Vietnam. On the night of 3 March 1969 the 16th Company, 4th Battalion, 202nd North Vietnamese Armoured Regiment attacked the US base at Ben Het with infantry, several PT-76 amphibious tanks and some BTR-50 troop carriers, with the aim of knocking out the M107 self-propelled 175mm guns stationed there. The base was defended by a couple of M42 Dusters and a platoon of M48A3s of Co. 'B', 1/69th Armor. At around 2100hrs, after artillery preparation, the North Vietnamese forces began their attack. The Pattons turned on their infra-red searchlights but these were ineffective due to ground fog. One PT-76 stumbled onto a landmine, but continued to fire. Using the PT-76's muzzle flashes as his aiming mark, Spec. 4

An M48A3 of 'M' Co., 3rd Sqn., 11th Cavalry churns forward during Operation 'Junction City' near Lai Khe, Vietnam, 13 April 1967. The M48A3 (Late Model) was the preferred Patton, since—unlike this vehicle—it was equipped with a G305 cupola vision riser which gave the commander better all-round vision. (US Army)

F. Hembree hit it with his second HEAT round, turning it into a fireball. A second PT-76 began firing at Sgt. Havermale's tank while the company commander, Capt. Stovall, was climbing aboard. A hit on the loader's hatch killed the loader and driver and blew Stovall and Havermale from the tank, but otherwise caused little damage. The tank of Spec. 4E. Davis blew a second PT-76 apart and heavy volleys from the five Pattons drove the NVA troops away after having lost two tanks and a BTR-50. The only other armoured vehicle confrontation in Vietnam occurred later in the war when an M728 Combat Engineer Vehicle mangled an NVA T-54 at close range with a single round of 165mm anti-bunker ammunition.

Vietnam

Until 1971 the ARVN (Army of the Republic of Vietnam) was equipped only with M41 light tanks in its armoured cavalry units. In July 1971 the first tank unit was formed—the 20th Tank Regiment, equipped mainly with left-over American M48A3s. The unit had a rather unique organisation, having an armoured rifle company which rode on the tanks to provide protection from anti-tank weapons. The ARVN crews initially had a great deal of trouble mastering the complex fire control system of the tanks, but by the time training was complete in the spring of 1972 this had been rectified. One of the most serious deficiencies of the unit was the lack of adequate armoured support equipment like AVLBs and M88 recovery vehicles, and this would cause losses in the later fighting.

In March 1972 the NVA launched its Easter offensive, with two tank regiments amongst the numerous units sweeping over the DMZ into South Vietnam's northern provinces. The ARVN 20th Tk. Regt. was rushed to the area in an effort to stem the NVA advance on Quang Tri. At the time the regiment had 44 M48A3 tanks, some in a poor state of repair, with a pronounced shortage of spare parts. On Easter Sunday, 2 April, the 1st Sqn. engaged a North Vietnamese armoured column from ranges of 2,500 to 3,000 metres, quickly destroying nine PT-76 tanks and two T-54s and breaking up the advance. Over the radio the NVA commander appeared baffled that he had been routed by a force he couldn't even see. It was ample testimony to the fact that the 20th Tk. Regt. had learned its lessons well. NVA attacks near Dong Ha were light until 9 April, when the 20th Tk. Regt. gutted another NVA attack by knocking out 16 T-54s and capturing a T-59 without loss to themselves.

A new element was introduced into the fighting on 23 April, when an M48A3 and an M113 ACAV were knocked out by 9M14M *Malyutka* guided anti-tank missiles. The NVA offensive resumed on 27 April with heavy artillery shelling, and 3rd Sqn. lost all its officers and three M48A3s to *Malyutka* missiles. By the following day the 20th Tk. Regt. had been reduced to only 18 tanks, but not before claiming five more NVA T-54s. By 2 May the regiment had lost all its tanks, some when they were unable to cross rivers, others to mechanical breakdowns, and many during intense fighting.

Following the 1973 ceasefire the 20th Tk. Regt. was re-formed along with two other units, the 21st and 22nd Tank Battalions, with M48A3 tanks. There were also a number of Patton companies formed which served with the ARVN armoured cavalry units. Although the South Vietnamese tankers proved to be more skilful than their NVA counterparts, during the 1975 invasion they were outnumbered in tanks by more than two to one and overwhelmed. Most of the tank units were lost in the initial fighting in the northern provinces and few of the 352 M48 and M41 tanks survived these battles.

An M48A3 (Late Model) of 2nd Ptn., 'C' Co., 1st Marine Tk. Bn. named 'Disaster', in action south-east of Danang, 12 February 1970. The track links provide a measure of stand-off armour against RPG-7s, and the commander's .50cal. machine gun has been remounted on the cupola roof for ease of operation. (USMC)

The Plates

A1: French M47, 8e Régiment de Dragons; Suez, 1956

Prior to embarkation for the Suez invasion French tankers scrounged some light sand-coloured paint to camouflage their equipment. There was not enough to go around, so only armoured vehicles were fully painted. The M47s retained the standard French serial number on the centre of the hull front and on the right hull upper rear. On the roof was painted a white 'H', standing for 'Hamilcar', the original name of the joint Anglo-French operation. The 'H' was used as an air identification marking, as it was feared that Egyptian armour would intervene. To serve as identification markings for the ground troops British and French tanks had a black band painted around the turret. The 8^{e} Dragons devised their own temporary unit insignia, a stylised sphinx and pyramid, which was painted on the turret sides in either red or blue. Above this and to the front was a red flaming grenade with the bridging weight number, '3' in black. Most of the M47s had matting stowed on the track guards for use should the tank become stuck in soft sand. Bands painted on the barrel probably identified companies.

An M48A3 (Late Model) supports 1/5th Marines during the bitter street fighting in the Imperial walled city of Hue, 12 February 1968. (USMC)

Most Patton units in Vietnam were equipped with the M48A3 since its use of diesel fuel made it less susceptible to mine-induced fires. However, heavy losses of tanks, particularly in the 1968 Tet offensive, led to the use of some M48A2s, like this one photographed in Quang Tri province during Operation 'Fisher' on 6 January 1969. (US Army)

A2: South Korean M47, DMZ, South Korea, 1974
This South Korean M47 is finished in a colourful pattern of bands over a basic olive drab base colour. First, white or very light cream coloured bands were applied, followed by a slightly rusty sand colour. No other insignia are evident. The South Koreans make extensive use of colourful, if not gaudy, pattern-painted camouflage. At least one M47 was painted in a scheme similar to this but with bright blue bands! The pattern shown here, or one without the cream stripes, was the most common pattern in the 1970s.

B1: Portuguese M47, Mecklenbourg Cavalry Regiment, 1st Independent Mixed Bde., 1973
This colourfully camouflaged M47 is finished in a pattern of No. 8 (24087) Olive Drab, No. 5 Earth Red and No. 4 Earth Yellow. The markings consist of the regimental crest in red and white on the turret sides; a town name carried on the glacis plate; and unit insignia, presumably indicating brigade and regiment, on the right and left fenders.

B2: Italian M47, Divisioni Corazzate 'Ariete', 1972
This M47, painted in overall Olive Drab, carries a typical array of the intricate markings usually found on tanks of the post-war Italian Army. The serial is carried as a narrow rectangle on the glacis plate, and as a stubbier rectangle on the upper right hull rear as shown in the inset drawings. Above the serial on the glacis plate is a standard NATO bridging circle giving the vehicle weight. The large white St Andrew's crosses are summer manoeuvre markings and are usually applied with

The 'Steel Tigers'—Co. 'B', 1/77th Armor—take up defensive positions near Khe San, 23 June 1969. (US Army)

a removable tempera paint. On the left fender is the national tri-colour insignia, and on the right is the unit insignia. Samples of the unit insignia of other M47 regiments are shown in the inset drawings (from left to right): Div. Cor. 'Ariete' (with a small yellow ram's head); Div. Cor. 'Centauro' (with a small centaur on a diagonally divided shield); Brigata di Cav. 'Pozzuolo del Friuli' (with a knight on a yellow shield); Rgto. Cav. 'Lancieri di Montebello' (with a white Roman eight); Rgto. di Ft. 'Torino' (with a rampant bull on a diagonally divided shield); 1° Rgto. Granatieri di Sardegna (with a white and black crest); and IV° Batt. Cor. Carabinieri (with a flaming silver grenade). The insignia on the turret side follows the same practice as during the Second World War—the colour indicates company (1st: red, 2nd: pale blue, 3rd: yellow, 4th: green) and the number of stripes inside the rectangle indicates the platoon. In this case the insignia indicates the 2nd Platoon, 2nd Company.

C1: Iranian M47M, Khuzestan front, 1980

This Iranian M47M is in the finish typical of

Iranian tanks taking part in the fighting with Iraq along the Shatt-al-Arab in 1980. This rear view clearly shows the extent of the modification work on the modernised M47M version. The vehicle is painted overall in a light sand colour, and the only marking evident is the national tri-colour roundel.

C2: Pakistani M47, 1st Armoured Division; Asal Uttar, 1965

According to Pakistani tankers, armoured vehicles in the 1965 fighting were almost invariably finished in their original paint schemes. In the case of the M47 this would have been US Olive Drab 24087. On some occasions a rough application of sand paint was added, but more often mud was applied in irregular patterns, as here. The basic vehicle markings are a turret number on the sides and rear, in this case '39', and a serial number on the hull front and rear as shown in detail in the inset drawing. This serial was sometimes also painted on the side of the hull stowage box. Bands were sometimes painted on the barrel to indicate company or platoon, but are obscured in this case by the mud. The Urdu numbering system is shown in the inset drawings, running from one to ten. The insignia of the division, a mailed fist on a divided square, was not normally seen in combat but was reserved for peacetime use, usually on the fender. Some M47s had their turret numbers painted in yellow or red with a white trim, probably to indicate battalion, and on a few vehicles the Urdu tactical numbers were sometimes supplemented with an Arabic two-digit numeral further aft on the turret, which usually did not match the Urdu number. Its significance is not known. Thanks are due to Charles Perkins and George Balin for information on which this illustration was based.

D1: Jordanian M47, 'C' Squadron 12th Tank Regiment; Jenin, 1967

Like most Jordanian armour in the 1967 fighting, the M47s were finished in an overall scheme of 34087 Earth Yellow with sprayed 24087 Olive Drab bands. The markings consisted of a name on the turret in black, 'Saib-bin-Ambr'; an army serial number and licence plate on the left front mudguard, with the Arabic word 'Al-Jaish' (Army) above and the number below; and a squadron insignia, a red circle in the British fashion, on the rear turret side.

D2: Belgian M47, 6ᵉ Régiment de Lanciers; Belgium 1967

Belgian M47s were finished in overall US Olive Drab 24087 or its equivalent. The vehicle serial number was carried in a white rectangle preceded by the national tri-colour on the bow and right upper hull rear. Above this was the standard NATO yellow bridging circle. Regimental insignia were usually carried forward on the turret

Pattons were frequently used for convoy duty in Vietnam. After this vehicle was hit by RPG-7s with some crew casualties, the rest of the crew erected a sand-bag parapet around the turret roof to offer better protection against close-range grenade attacks. This M48A3 served with 3/4th Cavalry supporting the 25th Inf. Div. in July 1968. (Col. James Loop)

sides, as is the case of the rampant bull insignia of the 6e Lanciers shown here. Insignia for other M47 regiments shown in inset (left to right) are 1er Régiment de Guides, 3e Régiment de Lanciers and 5e Régiment de Lanciers. The 6e Lanciers, which was attached to the 1er Division d'Infanterie, carried the divisional insignia on the right fender —this is repeated in detail in an inset drawing.

E1: Pakistani M48, 6th Armoured Division; Sialkot sector, 1965

The M48 shown in this illustration carries much the same style of markings as the M47 shown in plate C2. Here, the mud bands are somewhat more distinct, and the serial number is carried on the side stowage box as well as the hull front and rear. The three barrel bands probably indicate 'C' Squadron, and the tactical number '12' a tank of the 1st Platoon. Some Pakistani tanks carried a white band around the turret as a means of distinguishing them from Indian tanks. This practice did not become widespread until the 1971 war, when both sides were using much the same equipment. Though not evident in this view, this particular vehicle was fitted with the rear hull rack for carrying additional 55gal. fuel drums.

E2: Spanish M48A1, Regimiento Alcazar de Toledo; Spanish Sahara, 1974

During the troubles in the Spanish Sahara in 1974 a battalion of M48 tanks from the Regimiento Alcazar de Toledo was sent from Madrid to bolster the Spanish garrison there. The markings are much the same as those used in Spain, but a hasty coat of sand paint was applied over the basic olive drab finish. On the turret side is a tactical number in white indicating 1^{a}Seccion, 2^{a}Compania, and the barrel bands also indicate the second company. On the bow is the divisional insignia of Division Acorazada 'Brunete' n.º 1 (DAC) with which this regiment serves when

stationed in Spain.

M48A3s of 'C' Co., 2/34th Armor move through the Filhol Plantation on a search and destroy mission, 18 January 1967. The M48 was preferred to the M551 due to its better mobility through dense foliage and its better protection against mines. The 2/34th Armor used playing card symbols on their Pattons, in this case the ace of spades. (US Army)

F1: Israeli M48A2C, 7th Armoured Brigade, Ugda Tal; Sinai 1967

The Israeli Pattons during the Sinai fighting were painted in the usual Israeli 'sand grey' colour (FS 36350—Methuen 5E3). The forward-pointing chevron on the turret side is believed to indicate 2nd Company, and the Hebrew letter *gimel* on a detachable canvas sheet indicates the third vehicle of its platoon. This tank carried the Hebrew letter *aleph* on the left rear fender, identifying it as a tank of the 79th Tank Battalion. Serial numbers, preceded by the Hebrew letter *tsadi*, are carried on the bow and on the upper front of the turret sides. Since these vehicles were ex-Bundeswehr they have German-pattern headlights and guards rather than the American variety.

F2: West German M48A2C, Pz.Btn. 364, 12.Panzer-Division, 1978

Tanks of the Bundeswehr are finished in a dark olive drab similar to the American variety. This vehicle has the usual Maltese cross on both turret sides; the 12.Panzer-Division patch on the hull front in red and black; the tactical number '233' (for 2.Kompanie, 3.Zug 3rd tank) behind the cross; a NATO bridging circle on the lower right lip of the bow; and a military serial prefixed in 'Y' preceded by the national tri-colour. This insignia is usually repeated in a similar fashion on the hull rear or fender. On the left front mudguard is a typical German-pattern map-derived tactical symbol, giving the battalion and company numbers. German Pattons were eventually fitted with an enclosed stowage bin like that used on the Leopard 1; and on this vehicle a white tactical insignia was painted on it, as shown in the inset drawing. The red cloth crosses on the turret side and hull front are used during summer manoeuvres to represent the 'red' attacking force for NATO wargames. German Pattons are usually fitted with AEG Telefunken searchlights rather than the American types; and this particular vehicle is equipped with a DWS-2 Talissi Laser Simulator Array, the most obvious features of which are the K. Eichweber pyrotechnic array above the barrel, and the orange 'bubblegum' light on the turret rear, which indicates when the tank has been 'killed'.

G1: USMC M48A3, 1st Marine Tank Battalion; Operation 'Badger Tooth', Quang Tri, Vietnam, January, 1968

Marine tanks are finished in overall FS 24052 Forest Green, which is distinctly greener that the US Army Olive Drab. This vehicle carries a personal name, 'Tula', on the gun barrel as well as a personal insignia, a white Maltese cross, on the canvas searchlight cover and on the bow. Marine insignia are usually painted in FS 23538 Yellow, and this includes the battalion shield, the company letter 'C' and the tactical number '34'. The tactical number and the 'C' definitely identifies this as a tank of Charlie Company. The battalion shield officially had the inscription '1 TK' in white with black trim, but for legibility and ease of stencilling it was often applied in Vietnam in red paint. This insignia was carried on the air filter sides, sometimes on the bow, and on the fuel and water cans to prevent pilfering and 'permanent loans'.

G2: US Army M48A3, 1st Battalion, 69th Armor; Ben Het, Vietnam, March 1969

This Patton is finished overall in Olive Drab

A superb character study of the Patton in Vietnam. This M48A3 (Late Model) covering the 101st Airborne Div. near the 'Rockpile' in I Corps, 13 March 1971, is amply equipped with extra .50cal. ammunition stowed on the fenders, along with 'C'-rations and other stores. Chain link fence was widely used by armoured units in defensive positions to protect against RPG-7s. The wire could prematurely detonate the incoming rocket grenade, and in some cases the grenade head would pass through one of the openings, where its fins would then catch. (US Army)

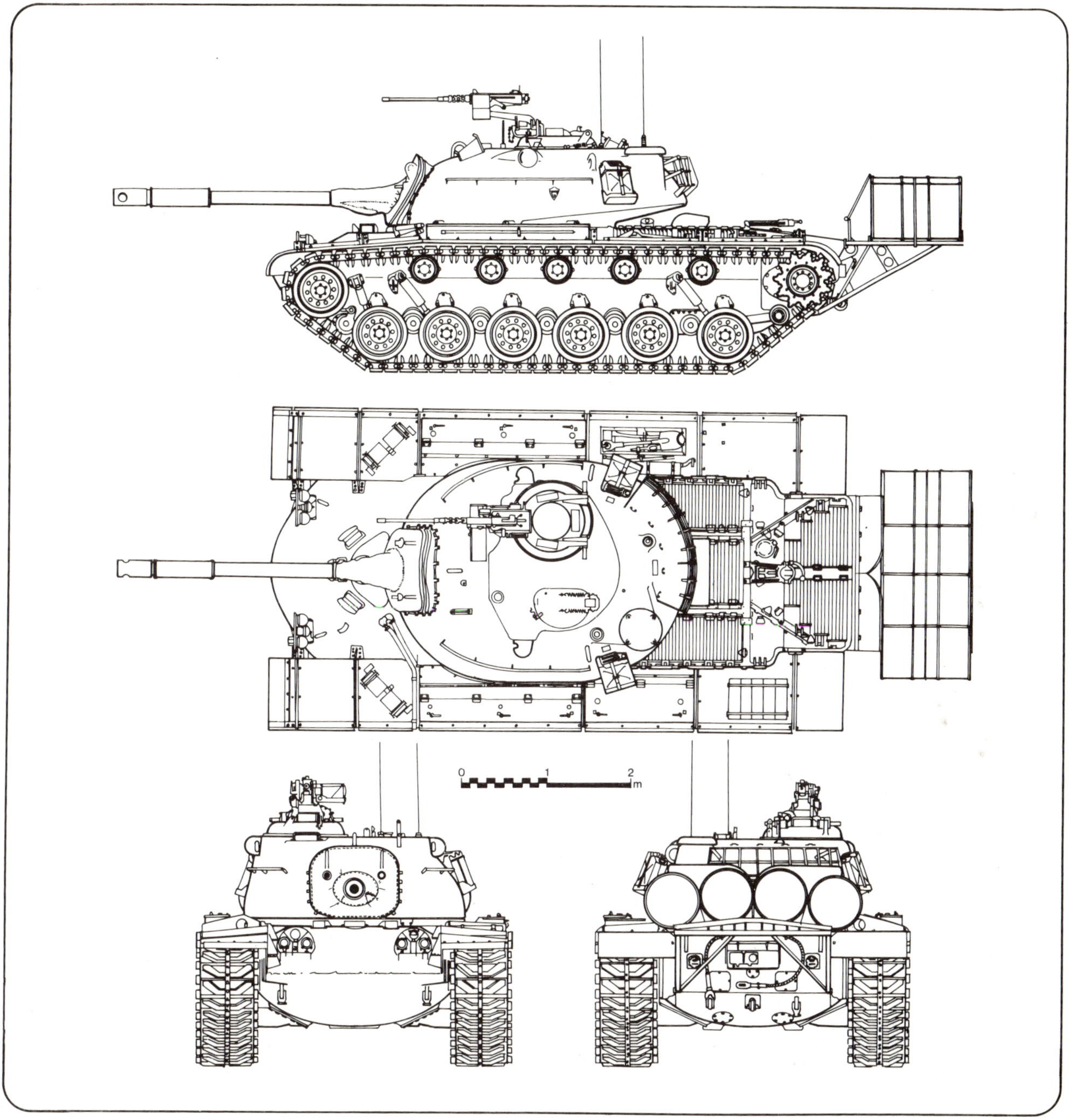

paint, badly faded and encrusted with dried mud and dust. From experience, the 1/69th Armor painted their tactical insignia high on the turret side, where it was less likely to become covered by spare track links used as stand-off armour. The square indicates 'A' Company, the standard Army pattern at the time being HQ Company (triangle), 'A' Company (square), 'B' Company (circle) and 'C' Company (diamond). Judging from the three barrel bands, this is a vehicle of the

Plan in 1/76 scale of Tank, Combat, Full-Tracked M48 (Steven Zaloga)

third platoon. Most tanks in Vietnam carried the standard US Army bumper codes, but in this case they are covered in mud. The US Army serial is evident on the side stowage bin.

H1: USMC M48A3, 4th Marine Tank Battalion; Fort Irwin, California 1980

Marine armour began adopting the Army's four-colour MERDC patterns in the mid-1970s; here the pattern is of Sand, Field Drab, Earth Yellow and Black with the two first colours predominating. Several tank battalions operating in California have occasionally carried this palm tree emblem, obviously derived from the old Afrika Korps insignia, while on desert training at Ft. Irwin, California. Marine units like the 3rd and 4th Tank Battalions have the Marine anchor-and-globe insignia in the centre, while Army units with their M48A5s (like National Guard Tank Battalions) use a black star instead. The insignia is usually applied on the turret sides behind the range-finder domes, and on the bow.

H2: South Korean M48A5 (Korean Pattern), Seoul, 1980

This illustration shows the Korean variation of the US Army MERDC patterns, these colours being Forest Green, Field Drab, Black and Sand. The only insignia is a Korean inscription on the right fender and the numeral '7' on the left. The three signal flags were prominently displayed for parade purposes.

Notes sur les planches en couleur

A1: Les marquages de reconnaissance des Alliés pendant cette campagne étaient un 'H' sur le volet de tourelle et une bande noire autour. Le sphynx et la pyrammide étaient les signes particuliers de ce régiment. **A2:** Camouflage bigarré typique des tanks sud-coréens—un M47 avait une harmonie similaire mais avec du bleu vif au lieu de marron.

B1: Armoiries du régiment sur les côtés de la tourelle; le nom du tank—un nom de ville—sur le glacis, et les symboles de brigade et de régiment sur les pare-chenilles. **B2:** Vue détaillée du style de marquage du numéro de série à la caisse arrière. La croix blanche est un marquage temporaire au cours de manoeuvres. Le tricolore national est sur le pare-chenille gauche et l'insigne d'unité à droite. Une autre vue détaillée montre des marquages d'unité différents. Voir le texte anglais.

C1: Comme d'habitude, les chars iraniens ne portent pas de marquages à part la cocarde nationale. **C2:** Traces de boue couvrant la peinture vert-olive. Numéro '39' sur les côtés de la tourelle et derrière. 'Poing de mailles', insigne de la division, ne figurait pas en action d'habitude. Les détails montrent les nombres de 1 à 10 en Urdu.

D1: 'Saib-bin-Ambr' inscrit sur la tourelle; notez le marquage d'escadron de style anglais, ici le cercle de l'escadron 'C'. **D2:** Insigne régimental sur le côté de la tourelle avant; les autres vues détaillées sont, de gauche à droite: 1er Guides, 3ème Lanciers, 5ème Lanciers. Signe de la lère Division d'infanterie sur le pare-chenille droit; cette unité en faisait partie.

E1: Trois bandes autour du canon indiquent probablement l'escadron 'C' et le numéro 12, un char du ler Peloton. La plupart des Pattons pakistanais portaient une rayure blanche autour de la tourelle en 1971 pour les différentier des Pattons de l'armée indienne. **E2:** Camouflage couleur de sable exécuté à la hâte semble indiquer que cette unité a été envoyée d'urgence au Sahara espagnol. Le chiffre de la tourelle indique la lère Section, 2ème Compangnie; les bandes du canon indiquent la compagnie; l'insigne du glacis est celui de la division—'Brunete'.

F1: Le chevron de la tourelle pourrait identifier la 2ème Compagnie; la lettre hébreue 'gimel' sur la toile signale le troisième char du peloton. La lettre 'aleph' sur le pare-chenille identifie le 79ème Bataillon de Chars. **F2:** Insigne rouge et noir de la 12ème 'Panzer Division' sur le glacis; '233' sur la tourelle indique le deuxième char, 3ème peloton, 3ème Compagnie du régiment. Sigle de bataillon/compagnie sur le pare-chenille gauche avant. Les croix rouges sont des marquages de manoeuvres.

G1: Les marquages 'Tula' et la croix de Malte sont individuels. Les marquages jaunes des Marines comprennent l'initiale 'C' de compagnie, le nombre 34 du char au sein du bataillon et le sigle en forme de bouclier du bataillon. **G2:** Le carré sur la tourelle indique la Compagnie 'A' et les trois bandes de canon identifient le 3ème peloton.

H1: Camouflage en quatre couleurs, instauré vers 1975, ici en harmonie de désert. Notex le sigle palmier, emprunté à le *Deutsches Afrika Korps*, et porté de manière non-officielle par des unités, s'entraînant en manoeuvres de désert; les Marines ajoutent l'insigne des USMC; les unités de l'armée ajoutent une étoile noire. **H2:** Version sud-coréenne du camouflage à quatre couleurs de l'armée américaine.

Farbtafeln

A1: Weisses 'H' auf dem Turmdach und schwarzes Band um den Turm waren die Erkennungsmarkierungen der Alliierten in diesem Feldzug. Sphinx- und Pyramidenabzeichen waren eine Eigenart dieses Regiments. **A2:** Farbenfrohe Tarnung, typisch für südkoreanische Panzer—einer der M47 zeigte ein ähnliches Schema, jedoch ersetzte ein leuchtendes Blau das Braun.

B1: Regimentales Wappen an den Turmseiten; Panzername, der einer Stadt, auf der Glacisplatte; und die Symbole der Brigade und des Regiments auf dem Kettenschutz. **B2:** Die detailierte Ansicht zeigt die Art der Seriennummermarkierung auf der oberen rechten Hinterseite des Rumpfes. Das weisse Kreuz ist eine vorübergehende Markierung für Manöver. Nationale Trikolore am linken Kettenschutz und Einheitsabzeichen rechts. Andere detailierte Ansichten zeigen verschiedene Einheitsmarkierungen—siehe Text in englischer Sprache.

C1: Typisch, iranische Panzer sind unmarkiert, ausser dem nationalen Kokardensymbol. **C2:** Lehm ist über die olivgrüne Farbe geschmiert. Die Turmnummer '39' ist auf den Seiten und hinten. Das 'Eiserne Faust' Divisionsabzeichen wird normalerweise nicht im Kampf getragen. Die Einzelheiten zeigen Urdu Nummern, 1 bis 10.

D1: Turmname 'Saib-bin-Ambr'; und bemerke die Schwadronenmarkierung im britischen Stil, hier der Kreis des 'C' Schwadron. **D2:** Regimentsabzeichen an der Turmseite, ziemlich weit vorne; andere in der detailierten Ansicht gezeigt sind (von links nach rechts) 1er Guides, 3^e^ Lanciers, 5^e^ Lanciers. Das Zeichen der 1. Infanteriedivision, welcher diese Einheit angeschlossen war, ist auf dem rechten Kettenschutz.

E1: Die drei Bänder um das Rohr zeigen wahrscheinlich das 'C' Schwadron und die Nummer '12' einen Panzer des 1. Zuges an. Im Jahr 1971 trugen die meisten Pakistani Pattons einen weissen Streifen um den Turm, um sie von den Pattons der indischen Armee zu unterscheiden. **E2:** Die hastig aufgetragene sandfarbene Tarnfarbe zeigt an, dass die Einheit in grösster Eile zur spanischen Sahara geschickt wurde. Die Turmnummer zeigt den 1. Zug, 2. Kompanie an; die Rohrbänder zeigen die Kompanie an; das Abzeichen auf der Glacisplatte ist das der Division—'Brunete'.

F1: Die Winkel auf dem Turm mögen die 2. Kompanie anzeigen; der hebräische Buchstabe 'gimel' auf einer Plane zeigt den dritten Panzer innerhalb eines Zuges an. Der Buchstabe 'aleph' auf dem Kettenschutz lässt das 79. Panzerbataillon erkennen. **F2:** Rot und schwarzes Abzeichen der 12. Panzerdivision auf der Glacisplatte; die Nummer '233' am Turm zeigt den zweiten Panzer, 3. Zug, 3. Kompanie des Regiments an. Bataillon/Kompanie Symbol auf dem linken vorderen Kettenschutz. Rote Tuchkreuze sind Manövermarkierungen.

G1: 'Tula' und Malteserkreuz sind persönliche Markierungen. Gelbe Marine-Markierungen beinhalten den Anfangsbuchstaben der 'C' Kompanie, den Panzer innerhalb eines Bataillons Nummer '34' und das Bataillonsabzeichen in der Form eines Wappenschildes. **G2:** Das Quadrat am Turm zeigt die 'A' Kompanie und die drei Bänder um das Rohr den 3. Zug an.

H1: Vierfarbentarnung, eingeführt in den Mitt-1970ern, hier in der 'Wüsten' Kombination. Bemerke das Palmenabzeichen, dem Deutschen Afrika Korps entliehen, inoffiziell von Einheiten beim Wüsten-training vorgezeigt—die 'Marines' fügten das USMC Abzeichen Die Armee-Einheiten den schwarzen Stern hinzu. **H2:** Südkoreanische Abart der US-Armee Vierfarbentarnung.